Greater Than a Tourist San Diego California USA

50 Travel Tips from a Local

>TOURIST

Alec Morse

>TOURIST

Order Information: To order this title please email lbrenenc@gmail.com or visit GreaterThanATourist.com. A bulk discount can be provided.

Lock Haven, PA

All rights reserved.

ISBN: 9781521404263

DEDICATION

This book is dedicated to my parents for choosing to stay in this beautiful city that I call home.

BOOK DESCRIPTION

Are you excited about planning your next trip? Do you want to try something new while traveling? Would you like some guidance from a local? If you answered yes to any of these questions, then this book is just for you.

Greater Than A Tourist – San Diego, by Alec Morse, offers the inside scope on San Diego.

Most travel books tell you how to travel like a tourist. Although there's nothing wrong with that, as a part of the Greater than a Tourist series this book will give you tips and a bunch of ideas from someone who lives at your next travel destination.

In these pages you'll discover local advice that will help you throughout your stay. Greater than a tourist is a series of travel books written by locals.

Travel like a local. Get the inside scope. Slow down, stay in one place, take your time, get to know the people and the culture of a place. Try some things off the beaten path with guidance. Patronize local business and vendors when you travel. Be willing to try something new and have the travel experience of a lifetime.

By the time you finish this book, you will be excited to travel to your next destination. Ten cents of each book purchased is donated to teaching and learning.

CONTENTS

CONTENTS

ACKNOWLEDGMENTS

Author Bio

WELCOME TO > TOURIST

1. Picking A Time To Visit San Diego

2. Packing For Your Trip

3. Getting To San Diego

4. Getting Around San Diego

5. Finding The Perfect Place To Stay

6. Remember These Safety Tips

7. Enjoy The Local Beers

8. Enjoy The Local Wines

9. Soak Up The Sun At The Best Beaches

10. Hike Through The Area

11. Visit The World Famous San Diego Zoo

12. Visit The Also Famous San Diego Safari Park

13. Build Memories At Legoland

14. Get Wet At SeaWorld

15. See More Aquatic Life At The Birch Aquarium

16. Watch The Seals At La Jolla Children's Pool

17. Ride The Rides At Belmont Park

18. Enjoy Some Water Sports At Mission Bay

19. Try Your Hand At Surfing

20. See A Beautiful Sunset From A Balloon

21. Ride A Horse On The Beach

22. Pull Out Your Clubs For These Great Courses

23. Slow Things Down By Going To The Theater

24. Take In The Sights Of The Infamous Balboa Park

25. Experience San Diego History At Old Town

26. Tour These Incredible Ships

27. Cruise The San Diego Harbor

28. Visit These Great Beachside Bars

29. Attend A Baseball Game

30. See Some Classic Horse Racing

31. Enjoy These Other Professional Sports

32. Get Some Food At A Local Farmers Market

33. Test Your Gambling Skills

34. Hit The Gaslamp Quarter For San Diego Nightlife

35. Do Other Stuff Downtown

36. Try These Restaurants When On A Budget

37. Find Other Great Places To Eat

38. See Some Incredible Art

39. Smell The Flowers At The Carlsbad Flower Fields

40. Walk Around The Historic Lighthouse

41. Relax On The Incomparable Coronado Island

42. Get The Most Out Of The Small Town Of Julian

43. Spend The Day At The San Diego County Fair

44. See The Many Parades And Fireworks

45. Test Your Bravery During Halloween

46. Traveling During The Winter Holidays

47. Catch These Not So Well-Known Sights

48. Handling A Sickness Or Emergency

49. Shop To Your Heart's Content

50. Stop And Talk To People

> Tourist

Author Bio

Alec Morse is a freelance writer who lives in San Diego, CA. Alec loves to rock climb, kayak, play tennis, read, and write.

Alec enjoys traveling all over the world and is partial to Australia and Europe. He lived in Guadalajara for two months in order to take in the Mexican culture, a huge part of present day and historical San Diego. To Alec, traveling is a natural urge of humans. People are meant to go on adventures, learn about new cultures, and appreciate different ways of thinking. In this day and age, moving around the globe has become so easy that it would be a waste to not take advantage of the many cars, trains, planes, or boats that can lead us to new and different places.

Alec was born in San Diego, went to college in Los Angeles, and then returned to San Diego. He loves the people, the vibe, the sights, and the weather of his great city.

How To Use This Book

This book was written by someone who has lived in an area for over three months. The author has made the best suggestions based on their own experiences in the area. Please check that these places are still available before traveling to the area. Get ready to enjoy your next trip.

WELCOME TO > TOURIST

Introduction

Welcome to the beautiful city of San Diego. There are few places in the world that offer continual great weather, a relaxed culture, and more things to do than someone could imagine. San Diego is a large city, but the county is incredibly spread out, offering a lot of recreational space and natural landscape amongst comfortable civilization. If you're looking for a place to find great food and drink, then this is the place to go. If you're hoping for tons of outdoor activities and excursions, then this is the right city. If you're searching for an area with friendly people and a stress-free lifestyle, then you have found it. If you just want to relax for a while in a sunny paradise on the beach, in the mountains, amongst the trees, or in the desert, then San Diego has what you need. Come to our wonderful city. My fellow San Diegans and I truly hope you enjoy your time with us.

1. Picking A Time To Visit San Diego

Honestly, there is no bad time to visit San Diego. That is one of the draws of this city: beautiful weather all year long. However, it does become colder towards November through February. Also, rain is not uncommon starting in the Winter and going through the Spring. During these seasons, it is important to look at the forecast in order to know what to expect. If you are planning to travel during a holiday, then be prepared for extra traffic on the roads (especially on the I-5 and I-15) and extra costs for flights. During the Summer, crowds are at a maximum. Beaches are one of the most crowded areas. If your time is flexible, then I would suggest coming during mid to late Spring or the beginning of Fall, that way the weather is still wonderful but crowds are not to be expected.

2. Packing For Your Trip

San Diego is the city of eternal sun (however, this rule is broken from time to time). Most locals can be seen wearing sandals, board shorts, and t-shirts. In cooler weather, it is not uncommon to see people in sandals, shorts, and a sweater. Some cultures frown upon wearing sandals as normal shoes, but it is very acceptable in San Diego. Hats are encouraged because the sun can be powerful, and sunscreen is certainly recommended. Also, sunglasses are a great thing to bring (get ones with UV protection) and you will fit right in with the locals. Most hotels will have towels you can take to the beach, though it is also recommended to bring bathing suits and your own towels to avoid any hassle. If you plan on going out, then some dressy clothes are recommended. While the majority of places do not have a dress code, most people dress to impress (and who doesn't love getting dressed up). If you have children, then it may be fun to bring some outdoor toys (Frisbee, football, etc.) since the city is full of parks and beaches with active people enjoying the sun. If you forget something or find that there is an item you want, San Diego is full of places to pick up anything you may need.

3. Getting To San Diego

There are numerous ways of traveling into San Diego. As a local, and a personal fan of driving, I use my car almost all the time. Coming from the East is easy if you use the I-8, which hardly has any traffic on it. Coming from the North, the I-5 is a large freeway with a beautiful view of the coast, though it is often congested since it is between two of the largest cities in California (Los Angeles and San Diego). The I-15 is another large freeway that heads into San Diego from the North and is much less traveled, offering beautiful mountain scenery and plenty of places to stop along the way. A great alternative to driving – offering convenience, comfort, and spectacular sights – is the Pacific Surfliner Train, by Amtrak. It travels from San Louis Obispo, to Santa Barbara, to Los Angeles, and all the way into San Diego (with many stops along the way). I have taken it many times and truly enjoy the ride. For those traveling on a budget, try using a bus system like the Greyhound, which offers cheap tickets, tons of travel times, and a wide variety of bus stop locations. For those coming from further away, San Diego International Airport recently underwent a renovation and is even more beautiful and efficient than before.

4. Getting Around San Diego

Once in San Diego, traveling is very easy. If getting around by car (whether in your own or renting one), I suggest using your personal GPS or picking up a map in order to navigate the many freeways in the area. The trolley system travels from East County all the way through downtown and is only $5 for a day pass. The Pacific Surfliner Train can also be used to get up and down the San Diego coast. Uber and Lyft are extensively used in the city, both convenient and inexpensive options. I would avoid using taxis because they are expensive, though the drivers are often knowledgeable and friendly. If you are the active type, I suggest renting a bike from a shop or using DecoBike, a system in San Diego where you can pick up a bike from one of the many stations and then drop it off at any other station. More about this system and the station locations can be found on the DecoBike website. A final tip for traveling in San Diego is to download the Compass Cloud App. This phone app allows you to buy and use tickets for buses, the trolley, and all trains around San Diego, eliminating the need to carry tickets or use the kiosks.

5. Finding The Perfect Place To Stay

Searching for a place to spend the night in San Diego comes down to many factors: the part of the city in which you are staying, the kind of accommodation you want, the activities in which you are interested, and your price range. I enjoy going on staycations (where I vacation in my home city) and have enjoyed staying at the hotels downtown. There are tons to choose from, they are in a very central location, and every one offers something unique. If you want something more like a resort, then take a look at the Omni La Costa Resort & Spa (known for its golf course and world renowned Chopra Center), the Fairmont Grand Del Mar (continually voted one of the best luxury resorts), the Rancho Bernardo Inn (secluded and elegant), and the Hotel Del Coronado (the backdrop for numerous Hollywood films and built in 1888). Airbnb is also a great choice when searching for deals and looking to live like a local.

6. Remember These Safety Tips

San Diego is a large city and like any large city, there are some people that don't mean well. These people are incredibly rare near the beaches and North County, but can appear when you are downtown. The homeless population tends to be appreciative of people that offer to help them and don't give anyone too much trouble, though be on the lookout for those that are trying to scam tourists by selling them false tickets to concerts or offering a deal that seems too good to be true. I, personally, have never had any trouble while in San Diego. Though I don't go looking for trouble and if it gets late, I am aware of my surroundings. Don't leave valuables visible in your car and if a situation feels wrong, then calmly remove yourself. With that said, the vast majority of people in San Diego are incredibly friendly and if you need help at any time, I encourage you to stop someone and ask for help. We value tourists in this city and truly want you to enjoy your time with us.

7. Enjoy The Local Beers

San Diego is well known for its beers, sometimes referred to as the beer capital. There are well over 100 breweries in the city (even more will have opened up by the time this book is published) and every one of them is delicious. The big names (which put our beer scene on the map) are Stone Brewery, Ballast Point, Greenflash, and Karl Strauss. Mission Brewery is the oldest in the county and for those that are truly beer freaks, my favorite spot is White Labs, where the employees are not beer tenders, but scientists. Please be careful; do not drink and drive. It is easy to get carried away with how much you drink and not realize you are over the limit. Most breweries and beer events offer deals for Designated Drivers, where you get free coffee and sodas. Just ask. Also, look into doing a tour or hiring a party bus that will take you to the breweries, thus eliminating the need to drive. For a truly unique experience, try the Social Cycle, a human powered pub party bike.

8. Enjoy The Local Wines

If wine is more your speed, then San Diego has some incredible offerings for you to enjoy. Temecula Valley is the up and coming wine scene, competing with (and often times beating) Napa Valley wines in competitions. However, wine aficionados are learning this and Temecula is becoming more and more crowded. A huge tip: after a day of wine tasting in Temecula, get on the freeway before 4pm. After 4, everyone rushes to the freeway and your travel time can easily triple. If you want a more private, quiet experience, hit some of the wineries in San Pasqual Valley (Orfila Winery is delicious and Cordiano Winery has arguably one of the best views in the county), or travel to Ramona where privately owned wineries are the norm. Industrial wineries are also growing in number, such as Carruth Cellars and the lesser known Koi Zen.

9. Soak Up The Sun At The Best Beaches

When one thinks of San Diego, one almost always imagines the beaches. And for good reason. The beaches are well maintained, exquisite in nature, and the weather is consistently perfect. If you want a beach with notoriety, then go to La Jolla Shores or Coronado. If you want to avoid the crowds, then try Torrey Pines and Del Mar. If you want acres of privacy, go to Imperial Beach near the border (it's really not as far as you think) or Silver Strand (miles of nothing but white sand). If you want tons of bars and restaurants near you, then Pacific Beach and Mission Beach (next to each other) are packed with things to do. When at the beach, be sure to locate the lifeguard towers and always do as they say. The lifeguards are good about warning bathers where rip currents are and how to stay safe. Also, one final (and important) tip. Paying for parking is silly. Every beach offers places to park for free. And if those are full, then try the nearby neighborhoods for street parking. You may end up with a five minute walk or so. Honestly, I can't remember the last time I paid to park at a beach in San Diego, even on holiday weekends. Though if you have some sort of accommodation or aversion to walking, then the paid parking lots are affordable and convenient.

10. Hike Through The Area

I am a huge fan of hiking and have traveled much of San Diego County on foot. The amount of trails and natural landscape are endless. A fun, easy hike is Torrey Pines State Reserve, with white rock bluffs and sensational ocean views. A more challenging hike is Iron Mountain in North County, with a full 360 degree view of the area from the top. If you enjoy hiking and swimming, Cedar Creek Falls is a great, secluded place with fresh water to swing into or jump into. It has become incredibly popular over the past few years and the government is now requiring permits for visitors. I see this as a good thing since it limits the number of people at the falls, and the permits only cost $10. If you want a lesser known area to hike, Lake Poway is home to fishing, boating, concerts, a bait shop that has a huge beer selection, and great hiking in the entire area. Potato Chip Rock is a must see. Go during the week and the place will be absolutely empty. For a large amount of natural area to explore, Mission Trails Regional Park is expansive. The newly built Visitor Center is astounding.

>TOURIST

>TOURIST

"Maui reminded me of San Diego: beautiful, but crowded." Larry Ellison

11. Visit The World Famous San Diego Zoo

Many times I have spoken with someone that is inherently or decidedly against the idea of a zoo. I usually tell them about the San Diego Zoo and they start to open their eyes to another way of thinking. I am in no way trying to change someone's opinion, though I am proving the point that the zoo in this city is world famous for one reason: it is different. The animals seem happy, they are in natural and large enclosures, the main focus is on conservation and rehabilitation rather than profits, and you don't get the sense that these animals are trapped. Parking at the zoo is free, the entrance fee is not very much, and the food is incredible (definitely have lunch at Albert's Restaurant). The earlier you go, the less people there will be. Everyone tends to arrive around 10am and then people start leaving in the late afternoon. There is enough time to see everything, but the park is very hilly and very big. It is easy to get fatigued. To avoid this, I suggest taking one of the bus tours (which run regularly) just to the right of the zoo entrance. They are informative and a good way to see many of the animals without any walking.

12. *Visit The Also Famous San Diego Safari Park*

The San Diego Zoo has a second park in the county: The Safari Park. This used to be a reproduction facility that started letting guests in years ago. It has grown into one of the most incredibly places you will ever see. The park is 1800 acres and its main draw is the expansive enclosures that include numerous African species roaming together like they would in the wild. There are tons of safaris to do (some where you can interact and feed the animals) and a tram that takes you around the enclosures. I actually worked here while I was in high school and have taken away nothing but positive experiences from the park. The animal encounters in the village are tons of fun. The Watering Hole is a great place to sit down, have some beer or wine, and watch the animals go by. My two favorite activities to do (they cost extra) are the Flightline Safari (where you literally fly over rhinos and gazelles and other animals) and the Jungle Ropes Safari (a challenging ropes course through the trees).

13. Build Memories At Legoland

Legoland is not just a place for children. I have gone multiple times in my adult life and have enjoyed every second of the San Diego park. The rides are certainly geared towards a younger crowd, though the incredible nature of the Lego sculptures is something you cannot miss. They have constructed entire cities out of those little blocks and the people that design the structures must have a great sense of humor. Every time I am there, I notice something new in the Lego cities (a car crash, someone proposing, a guy sitting on the toilet). It is all age appropriate and entertaining. Also, the Legoland Water Park is surprising well done. I was skeptical the first time I went, but it turned out to be a blast. Definitely do not miss the lazy river they constructed. It has specially designed inner tubes that park goers can connect large, foam Lego blocks to, allowing them to make their own designs and even link tubes together.

14. Get Wet At SeaWorld

Another great park that San Diego has to offer is SeaWorld. The company does a large amount of research and conservation for aquatic life around the globe, but they also operate a pretty fun theme park. It can be crowded in the summer, especially on weekends, but during the Fall and Winter the place is a ghost town. I have gone offseason before and been the only person on rollercoasters, with the operators letting me go around and around until I get sick. The downside is that this is when they do construction on enclosures (if needed) and Shipwreck Rapids (a large water ride) is not open during the Winter. However, it is a great way to skip the crowds. Manta, SeaWorld's newest rollercoaster, is a must do. As is Journey to Atlantis. Also, be sure to catch the Sea Lions LIVE show. The jokes are corny, but it's truly hilarious.

15. See More Aquatic Life At The Birch Aquarium

The Birch Aquarium, run by the University of California, San Diego, is an informative and beautiful look into ocean life on the West Coast. Many of the employees there are real oceanographers that truly know their stuff. However, if you're looking for more than just marine knowledge and pretty fish, check out their Green Flash Concert Series. The aquarium hosts some big name bands right along the water's edge. But be aware that most of these events are 21+. Also, I strongly recommend seeing the Infinity Cube: Language of Light. It is a large cube that surround guests with screens showing bioluminescent organisms reacting to various things. The show is pretty jaw-dropping. The aquarium closes early, at 5PM, so this is a good thing to do in the morning.

16. Watch The Seals At La Jolla Children's Pool

La Jolla Children's Pool is a place that attracts locals and tourists alike. It is a small beach, surrounded by natural rock and a walkable jetty that produces a secluded spot on which seals hang out. The area was built for children to swim but has since been taken over by the seals. Advocates for both sides are fighting for who has the right to the space, seals or children, which has created an interesting situation where both people and the seals are present on the beach. I suggest viewing the seals from a distance, giving them plenty of space (though they are accustomed to humans) and certainly do not swim in the water at Children's Pool. It can be dangerous and contaminated with seal feces. Pupping season runs from December to May, so this is a good time to head down and see some seal pubs being born on the beach. The jetty is a great place to walk, but beware of large waves. Us locals enjoy seeing tourists head onto the jetty during stormy seas and get drenched.

17. Ride The Rides At Belmont Park

Belmont Park is one of the few remaining oceanfront amusement parks from the early 1900s. It opened in 1925 and has been running strong ever since. It's free to walk around, though you must pay for the attractions. The main draw is the Giant Dipper Roller Coaster: a large, wooden roller coaster that has stood since the parks opening and is a National Historic Landmark. It may look sketchy, but the roller coaster is well maintained and well worth the price. You will bump and scream your way along the track with a smile on your face. After enjoying the rides and games, my favorite spot to eat near there is WaveHouse. The restaurant sits along the boardwalk and offers beach inspired seating in the sand, with tiki bars, cabanas, and fire pits. It has great food, great drinks, and you can watch people take on the wave machine.

18. Enjoy Some Water Sports At Mission Bay

My favorite spot in San Diego is Mission Bay. This aquatic park is a manmade lagoon that is fed from the ocean. The water is calm, making it the perfect location for all kinds of water sports. If you have your own craft (kayak, paddle board, sailboat, etc.) the best place to launch is at De Anza Cove, right by Mission Bay Park. It is easily accessed by the I-5 and has a huge parking lot that is never full (all parking around Mission Bay is typically easy and always free). A fun activity is paddle board yoga, done at the many rental places around the bay. Also, if you've ever wanted to try a water powered jetpack, then look no further than Mission Bay Sportcenter. Throughout the area, you can also find jet skiing, wake boarding, a boat with a hot tub on it (one of my favorites) and so much more. SeaWorld borders Mission Bay, and so sometimes I will kayak to the back of SeaWorld where their Cirque de la Mer Acrobatic Show meets the water, and watch the show for free. Take advantage of all that Mission Bay has to offer.

19. Try Your Hand At Surfing

San Diego is often attributed to shaggy, blond guys in sandals carrying surfboards, and this is not far from the truth. Tons of locals surf and even more people travel from afar to take advantage of the great surfing. There are countless places to rent surfboards at every beach and tons of these places offer surfing classes. If you are new to surfing, then I strongly recommend taking a class. The instructors are friendly and it is better to know what you are doing when dealing with something as powerful as the ocean. When in the water, remember that surfing is not a free-for-all. Share the waves with people. There is typically some sort of line of people waiting to catch a wave. If you are ever confused about something, feel free to ask the surfers around you. They welcome new comers and will appreciate you making the effort to understand surfing etiquette. Some good beaches at which to surf are La Jolla Shores, Windansea Beach, and Pacific Beach. These places have a great expanse of space for activities and great waves.

20. See A Beautiful Sunset From A Balloon

An unforgettable experience for couples, families, or friends is to watch the sunset from a hot air balloon. The best places to go are along the North County coast, at Solana Beach or Del Mar. There are numerous companies that offer balloon rides and I have never once heard of a bad experience from any of them. Sky's The Limit is a good company that offers a couple locations: one on the coast (Del Mar) and one inland (over the rolling green hills of Temecula). Be sure to bring warm clothes because it gets cold when you are soaring high through the sky as the sun is going down. And don't forget to take lots of pictures. Some companies allow you to bring food and wine, so definitely look out for that.

>TOURIST

"Broad, wholesome, charitable views of men and things cannot be acquired by vegetating in one little corner of the earth all of one's lifetime." – Mark Twain

21. Ride A Horse On The Beach

This is as cool as it sounds. A lesser known activity of San Diego, there are several ranches that offer horse riding on the beach. I have found that they are all located near the border, at Imperial Beach, which is surprisingly close to downtown San Diego but avoids all the crowds that typically gather on the beaches. I used the company Pony Land San Diego and had an absolutely wonderful time. It was a private tour for my friend and I (with a guide of course) and we spent a couple hours enjoying our time with the well-trained horses. They truly enjoy the water. If you let them, the horses will rush through the waves and go as deep as their necks, soaking your lower half. It is a great experience for groups or couples or to just take the family on a calm ride. Truly a unique adventure.

22. Pull Out Your Clubs For These Great Courses

Golf is a well-loved game in San Diego. With plenty of world class courses to choose from, there's no shortage of green. Some of the top, well-known courses are Oaks North, The Grand Golf Club, Fairbanks Ranch, Torrey Pines, Omni La Costa, and the Rancho Bernardo Inn. These courses are beautiful, difficult, and have hosted PGA tournaments before. They can get crowded and very expensive for this reason. If you are looking for lesser-known courses, then try Carmel Mountain Ranch and Mt. Woodson. In either case, it is helpful to call ahead and ask about the crowds at the course. The pro shop will tell you whether it is a good time to go or not.

23. Slow Things Down By Going To The Theater

The theater is not for everyone, though I strongly recommend it to those that enjoy plays, musicals, or concerts. The San Diego Symphony performs in Copley Symphony Hall, a beautiful theater that commands attention. Tickets can be cheap and shows are announced typically more than a year in advance. The musicals are straight from Broadway, showing in the Civic Theater downtown. The theater is small, so don't be afraid to save some money by getting seats in the balcony. There are tons of other small theaters (like The Old Globe, worth looking into), but one I really enjoy is the Organ Pavilion. Located in Balboa Park, it boasts the largest outdoor organ in the world and offers free concerts on Sundays at 2PM. During the summer, there are also concerts at 7:30PM on Mondays. The organists are talented and the music can be heard all around the park.

24. Take In The Sights Of The Infamous Balboa Park

Balboa Park has many things to offer, more than I can list in this book. For one, the museums are wonderful. The Fleet Science Center is interactive and has a great IMAX cinema. The Natural History Museum is beautiful and has numerous exhibits on animals and plants. The Museum of Man often has unique, rotating exhibits to always keep an eye on. The botanical garden is free to enter and located by a large, scenic koi pond. There are other museums and art galleries (I personally love the Model Railroad Museum), though just walking around the park is a blast. Street performers line the pedestrian roads, live music fills the air, and the history of the area is fascinating. For the first time in decades, you can climb to the top of the California Tower, which I highly recommend. A fun, hidden gem is the Spanish Village: an area of local artists selling their work. Rent one of the tandem bikes and cruise through Balboa Park in style.

25. Experience San Diego History At Old Town

The history of San Diego is deep and rich. Old Town transports visitors into a time before cars, before huge buildings, and before the West Coast was fully settled. All the buildings in Old Town are original, maintained throughout the years in an effort to preserve the fascinating history and culture of the past. My favorite restaurant in the area is Casa de Reyes (try the churros, trust me). Take the time to walk around the park and enjoy the couple hundred year old trees, the aging buildings, and the many shops selling unique souvenirs. For those interested in ghost hunting, the Whaley House is considered one of the most haunted places in the country (and the history behind it is pretty fascinating). For convenience and tours, hop on to one of the Old Town trolleys that carry passengers around the area. Parking is free, but can get full very quickly. I suggest taking the San Diego trolley into the park.

26. Tour These Incredible Ships

As a well-known military port, San Diego is home to many ships, those that are retired and those that are still in operation. The Maritime Museum has one of the largest collection of vessels, ranging from sail boats to steam boats to a submarine (and yes, you can explore all of these ships). On holiday weekends, the museum can be crowded, but almost any other time there will never be an issue with crowds. There isn't much parking by the museum, but if you park downtown or take the trolley into downtown, it is a quick walk to the harbor's edge. Also, while in the area, explore the USS Midway Museum. This is a retired aircraft carrier with old planes on it. I actually had my senior prom on the Midway and I have to say, it is one of the coolest ships to explore. Entrance is cheap and you can spend hours wandering around the entire vessel.

27. Cruise The San Diego Harbor

Cruising the harbor is a great event for anyone at any time. If you go during the day, you are sure to have beautiful weather and see many locals sailing through the waters. This will also give you a perfect view of the downtown skyline. You can also take evening and night cruises through the harbor, great options for dinner events or simply to take in the beautiful night sky. There are numerous companies that offer daily excursions, some cheaper than others (and you really do get what you pay for). I recommend looking at Hornblower. This is a big company that offers numerous options when choosing the perfect cruise. They are used by schools, companies, as well as private parties. They have short and long cruises and you can choose from different ships. For some unique cruises and tours, look at Flagship Cruises & Events. They have some themed tours and something called the Patriot Jet Boat Thrill Ride. It is just as much fun as it looks.

28. Visit These Great Beachside Bars

For me, there isn't much better than relaxing in a bar with the ocean right outside your window. Some of my favorite beachside bars are the 710 Beach Club (a great place to watch the baseball game), the PB Shore Club (with a massive outdoor patio to soak in the sun), and Guava Beach Bar & Grill (has a pool and a cool tiki theme). In general, Pacific Beach is a good place to go bar hopping next to the ocean. If you're looking for a family friendly restaurant on the beach, then try the Brigantine in Del Mar (a well-respected seafood chain), Baja Beach Café in Pacific Beach, and Coronado Brewing Company Brew Pub on Coronado Island (one of my favorite places to go). All of these venues can become very crowded at lunchtime, especially on weekends, so I recommend either getting reservations or showing up around 11AM (maybe a little later for the bars, though no one will judge you).

29. Attend A Baseball Game

Petco Park has been called the most beautiful professional baseball stadium. The park was built on the South side of downtown and incorporated some of the original buildings in the area into the design, bringing together new and old architecture. San Diegans are not known for their devotion to attending every game and so tickets are easy to come by. To save money, you can often purchase a cheap ticket for the nosebleeds and then find a better seat closer to the field. San Diego fans are incredibly friendly and rarely become too competitive. The food at the park is incredible, with many of the local restaurants being represented, and the beer selection is even better. I suggest going to an afternoon game because most people are at work and so the place is rarely crowded, and the weather is guaranteed to be wonderful. Getting to the park is easiest with the San Diego Trolley. It stops right at the entrance. The stadium does have a parking lot that fills up, but extra parking can be found at the Hilton, with a bridge leading directly from their parking lot to the stadium entrance.

30. See Some Classic Horse Racing

Horse racing is as exciting as it looks in the movies. The Del Mar racetrack has been in operations since 1937 and has hosted some major races in history. Even if horse racing is not your thing (it's not like I follow the sport religiously) the atmosphere of being at the races is truly one of a kind. Seeing the owners in their boxes, the jockeys mounting their horses, the well-dressed regulars holding their betting tickets, and feeling like you are a part of a different time period is truly incredible. Parking is cheap and easy, with plenty of spots for everyone. If you plan to see a race, I strongly suggest you try to make it to Opening Day, usually in the middle of July. Everyone dresses for the occasion and women bring their most stylish, elegant hats (there is even a contest) so it feels like you have been transported back to the 1940s.

>TOURIST

"To my mind, the greatest reward and luxury of travel is to be able to experience everyday things as if for the first time, to be in a position in which almost nothing is so familiar it is taken for granted." – Bill Bryson

31. Enjoy These Other Professional Sports

Maybe you are the kind of person that likes to watch sports, any kind of sports. The San Diego Gulls are part of the American Hockey League and tickets are cheap. I highly suggest going to a game if you enjoy hockey. But a tip: if getting beer, I would stick to purchasing bottled or canned beers from the arena. I have had numerous "bad" beers from uncleaned taps. The San Diego Soccer Club is also a great team and they may be getting a brand new stadium in place of the old Charger football stadium. Another great sport is Professional Ultimate Disc (just like in college), and the San Diego Growlers are a fun team. They're still gaining a following so games are not crowded and very relaxed. I suggest bringing a cooler with some drinks and food and enjoying the game. The La Costa Open is a professional tennis tournament where some of the greatest tennis pros come to play. San Diego State basketball is also a big deal.

32. Get Some Food At A Local Farmers Market

The county holds regular farmers markets every day of the week. A good way to find what markets are held where, and when, is to use the website sdfarmbureau.org and then clicking on "buy local" followed by "farmers markets". My favorites are the Little Italy farmers market on Saturdays and the Hillcrest farmers market on Sundays. Keep an eye out for some great wine and beer tasting opportunities at the markets. Mike Hess Brewery is often present at the Hillcrest one and Golden Coast Mead is always at the Little Italy one. It is helpful to bring your own reusable bags to the markets because some vendors don't have bags for you. Also, if you plan to spend the day walking around the area or traveling somewhere else, then I would bring an insulated bag or a cooler in order to keep the things you buy fresh.

33. Test Your Gambling Skills

What is a trip to California without hitting some casinos on Indian Reservations? San Diego is home to some great casinos that offer a wide range of games, restaurants, shops, and entertainment. For younger travelers, Barona and Sycuan casinos are both 18 and older. Valley View is 21 and older. Valley View Casino has an incredible buffet (though it can be pricey) and a hotel at which to stay. It is located in North County but can be difficult to get to during rush hour since there is a small highway that leads to it. Barona Resort & Casino is more of a destination than Valley View since it has a full resort with golf course, though it is also off the beaten path and can take a while to get to (out in East county). Sycuan Casino is off of the I-8 and has a full resort, hosting concerts as well. My favorite place to gamble is Viejas Casino and Resort. It is a little further East, though it has tons of things to do for the entire family. There are outlets, bowling, a resort, the casino, a roller rink, and a great amphitheater with some big name guests performing.

34. Hit The Gaslamp Quarter For San Diego Nightlife

My favorite place to go out for a drink is the Gaslamp Quarter. I hit this spot a couple times a year and it is always a blast. If you are looking for dinner or a show or just a couple drinks, then I suggest parking in the Horton Plaza Mall parking structure. It is in the Gaslamp Quarter, parking is very affordable, and there are always plenty of spots. If you are looking to drink yourself over the legal driving limit, then it is best to either take the Trolley into the area (there is a station for the Gaslamp) or get a ride there. Early in the night, I suggest hitting Vin de Syrah. It is a wine bar with an awesome Alice in Wonderland theme that is not crowded early in the evening, though it gets wild after 10PM. The place to go to when the area is packed with people is The Tipsy Crow. It has a cover but this limits the number of people in there. If you want a truly wild night, go to Double Deuces. It has a mechanical bull. There are tons of bars and restaurants, all walking distance from one another. I will sometimes just go bar to bar, trying each one out and seeing if it is offering the atmosphere that I am looking for that particular night. The area is incredible and should not be missed.

35. Do Other Stuff Downtown

There is so much to do in downtown San Diego. It is a beautiful destination any time of year, but is especially beautiful during warm, sunny days. Many people are in the bay on their boats, friendly San Diegans are walking the streets, and there is a world of opportunities before you. Seaport Village is a must see spot. It is a collection of shops and restaurants on the edge of the harbor with everything from a hot sauce store to a bizarre bookstore. Also downtown is the Horton Plaza mall, a great place to find brand name stores and food options. My favorite place to go is the San Diego Central library: recently constructed and absolutely beautiful on the inside and outside. If you get thirsty, stop at Mission Brewery. It has great beer (and some other drink options), plenty of space, and tons of great bar games.

36. Try These Restaurants When On A Budget

There are plenty of venues in San Diego that serve quality, delicious food while not emptying your wallet. Most restaurants downtown will be on the expensive end (some more than others) and so, to find cheaper food, the surrounding areas have some great options. Hillcrest is a great place to find great, affordable food, as is University Heights. My area of choice for inexpensive food is North Park, which has a large arts district that boasts tons of restaurants, all centered around University Ave. and 30th St. My standard process for picking a place to eat is to walk around an area populated with venues (like the ones above), and look at the menus that are on display outside the front door. Almost every restaurant will do this and you can decide if that particular place sounds good and is within your budget.

37. Find Other Great Places To Eat

If you are looking for some nicer places to eat and are not worried about a budget, then San Diego has some great options to choose from. Rather than listing them all, I will give you some areas at which to look that have some incredible restaurants. Downtown is full of great places to eat, like Ra Sushi, Morton's, Flemings, and Searsucker. There are many good restaurants lining the San Diego harbor, as well as the Mission Bay area. La Jolla Village has tons of incredible restaurants, like Karl Strauss, Herringbone (with an incredible interior design) and the Marine Room (a favorite of mine where the windows of the restaurant sit right on the beach, even taking huge hits from waves during high tide).

38. See Some Incredible Art

North Park has a great arts district complete with galleries and markets. Balboa Park is home to many museums that offer a wide range of art. The Timken Museum of Art is a beautiful building with rotating works and is free to the public. The San Diego Museum of Art is located in a beautiful building, as is the Museum of Photographic Art (for those into photography), and the Mingei International Museum is full of folk art from all over the world. To see some local artists, there are tons of conventions around the county where local artists show off – and sell – their craft. My favorite is the Mission Federal Art Walk in Little Italy, always at the end of April. It has every kind of art imaginable and the artists are incredibly welcoming, and happy to explain their process and muse to the public. It is a weekend event, so if you go on Saturday, then it coincides with the Little Italy Farmers Market.

39. Smell The Flowers At The Carlsbad Flower Fields

The flower fields in Carlsbad are a fantastic example of how traditions are preserved within San Diego. Starting in the 1950s, the flower fields are 50 acres of brightly colored flowers extending as far as the eye can see. It occurs between March and May. I would suggest going in the end of March or anytime in April because this is when the flowers are the biggest and the brightest. There are also rides and food for visitors. This is truly a unique adventure that can create some pretty incredibly family or couples photos.

40. *Walk Around The Historic Lighthouse*

There are two lighthouses within San Diego: the Old Point Loma Lighthouse and the New Point Loma Lighthouse. Both of them offer tours but it is obviously the old lighthouse that has more history. The old lighthouse is located within Cabrillo National Monument, another great place to visit with gorgeous, rolling green fields of the military cemetery. The history is fascinating and there are rarely large crowds. While at Point Loma, take a look at the tide pools on the West side of the point. Also, while on the peninsula, look directly South and you will see Mexico in the distance.

>TOURIST

>TOURIST

*"Afoot and lighthearted I take to the open road,
healthy, free, the world before me." – Walt Whitman*

41. Relax On The Incomparable Coronado Island

A secluded paradise within San Diego, Coronado Island is not technically an island. The bulk of it rests in the middle of the harbor, though a small strip of land connects the bulbous end to Imperial Beach (check it out on a map, it's pretty odd). Coronado is home to multimillion dollar homes, a fantastic shopping and dining district off of highway 75, and the famous Hotel Del Coronado. Stop by the East side of the island to get a perfect view of downtown San Diego from across the bay, and then cruise over to the West side where the beaches are massive and the resorts sit. I often hang out on the outdoor bar of the Hotel Del for a drink in the sun. During the winter, the Hotel Del puts up an ice skating rink right on the beach, a pretty surreal experience during the warm winters of San Diego. If you want a secluded beach on which to hang out, cruise down the Silver Strand where white sand sits on either side of the road and miles of beach stretch in front of you. For a great adventure, look up the Grunion Run schedule. You will not be disappointed.

42. Get The Most Out Of The Small Town Of Julian

Julian is the epitome of small towns. It rests in the mountains of East County and still maintains the mom and pop shops of times long ago. Parking is not too bad and always free, though I suggest bringing coins to pay for public restrooms. All restaurants and some stores have bathrooms, though they are reserved for paying customers. The public restrooms are numerous and clean, though coin operated. What we do is one person pays to enter the restroom, and then we just hold the door open for the next person. Julian is famous for its apples, and so the apple pies are mind blowing. Julian Pie Company in town can get very busy all the time, so I often stop at Mom's Pie House just outside of town for shorter waits. Every season is a good time to go, though Winter can get very crowded because Julian is often blanketed in snow. The drive out there is gorgeous every time of year, but be respectful of those that live off of the highway. Too many times I see people parking on the side of the road and playing in the snow on someone's farm. For obvious reasons, the owners don't like this. Park your car at Julian and walk around the surrounding area for some hiking adventures. In the Winter, always bring chains for your car.

43. Spend The Day At The San Diego County Fair

The San Diego County Fair (formerly called the Del Mar Fair because it is located at the Del Mar Racetrack) is the biggest county fair in the state. Every year has a different theme, with the grounds completely decorated to fit the theme, and the amount of things to do is incredible. The food is always unhealthy at the fair (a big selling point for visitors) so if you want healthy food, bring your own. The rides are fantastic and the shopping is endless. There are free concerts almost every day, as well as some concerts that require advanced tickets. The local art to view is pretty incredible. To save money, I suggest buying tickets at Vons or Albertsons, which help sponsor the fair every year. Also, rather than paying to park at the fair, I would park at what is called the Del Mar Horse Park. It is totally free, and there are regular, free shuttles that take you right to the front entrance of the fair. I enjoy this option not only because it is convenient and free, but the buses that take you are old, double decker buses that offer a great experience along the way.

44. See The Many Parades And Fireworks

During national holidays like the 4th of July, there are tons of places across the county that bring the public firework shows and parades. Most high schools will do some sort of fireworks performance as do the big amusement parks. During the Winter months, there are tons of parades to celebrate Christmas and other holidays. Gaslamp Quarter, La Jolla, and even the San Diego bay have some great parades. Mardi Gras, St. Patrick's Day, and LGBT Community all have parades that course through the city. SeaWorld has nightly fireworks shows during the summer, which can be seen from all across the area, and after a couple Padres Games during the summer there are fireworks. If you are looking to travel during some of these times, I suggest you look up when these events will be. For parades, get there really early in order to secure a spot along the route. For fireworks, just look up wherever you are and you can see them. I suggest finding a nice, rooftop restaurant or bar downtown to watch the SeaWorld or Petco Park fireworks from a comfortable and unobstructed seat.

45. Test Your Bravery During Halloween

Halloween is a big deal in San Diego and this is when all of the haunted houses come into existence. The Whaley House, considered one of the most haunted places in the country, does nightly ghost tours that really turn up the scare factor during Halloween. My favorite place to go is The Haunted Trails at Balboa Park. This is an outdoor walk through the woods where you can encounter abandoned school buses full of "dead" people, terrifying mazes, freaky cabins, and a guy holding chainsaw behind a tree. The fact that you are outside in natural darkness is pretty freaky. Another great option, and the longest running haunted house in San Diego, is the Haunted Hotel. This one is located downtown in the Gaslamp. There are tons of other options throughout the county, but these are the main three that people seek out.

46. Traveling During the Holidays

As a big city, San Diego can get incredibly busy during the holidays. Typically, Thanksgiving Eve, Christmas Eve, and New Year's Eve are terrible days to travel because so many people are on the road. On the actual holiday, most people remain inside and so the roads are very open. But like most places, the majority of stores are closed on holidays and so it is best to prepare ahead of time when buying food or drink. If you are interested in seeing Christmas lights, the San Diego Harbor is alight with tons of decorated boats. The Gaslamp Quarter is decked out in holiday gear, as is Old Town and Balboa Park. As far as residential areas, the best places to go are called the Griswolds (Stoutwood St., Poway), Christmas Card Lane (Ellingham St., San Diego), and Candy Cane Courts (Hickory, Butterwood, and Rockrose, Poway). The San Diego Zoo and Safari Park also have holiday lights and events at night. Flights into San Diego can be expensive at this time because the weather is often great (unlike other cities) and everyone is traveling. So if driving or taking the train is not an option, then be prepared to pay a little more.

47. Catch These Not So Well-Known Sights

There are a ton of things to see that are rarely shown in travel books or blogs. One neat place is Old Poway Park, the origins of the city of Poway with all original buildings, a museum, a blacksmith, an operational train on the weekends, a restaurant, and tons of park space for events. Soledad Mountain, in La Jolla, is a great place to visit that offers an unobstructed view of the entire city. There is plenty of parking and a war memorial at the top. Also in La Jolla, are the three troll bridges. This is an old legend told to children that there are three bridges in this particular neighborhood and if you find all three, trolls will come out from under the third bridge and kill you. Pretty dark. My father used to drive my sister and I (many, many years ago) around the area in search of the bridges. After finding two, we would get very nervous that we would soon find the third. However, there are only two bridges in the neighborhood so you never do find the third. Hence, the weird legend. The bridges are on Al Bahr Dr. and Castallena Rd. Even if you aren't into the story, the bridges are very strange and the area is absolutely beautiful. Another fun thing to do that some people don't come across is the House of Pacific Relations in Balboa Park. It is a series of small buildings, each one representing one of 33 countries, that is staffed with people from those countries. Each cottage holds events, has food, and information about the country.

48. Handling A Sickness Or Emergency

Things happen anywhere you go. It is important to remain relaxed and know that there are people there to help you. San Diego is a large city and so the services are wide-spread and top notch. In fact, San Diego has some of the best hospitals in the entire country, continually winning awards for their services. Wherever you end up staying, I suggest you look up the closest hospital just in case. However, for something that is not an emergency but still urgent (like a deep cut or illness), there are Urgent Cares all over the county that are much cheaper and more appropriate. Like all US cities, the number to call for emergencies is 911, and the dispatcher will take good care of you. For roadside assistance, AAA is heavily used in San Diego and a great option. If you don't have this, then there are numerous companies in the area that will be happy to help. I suggest you look up some companies and their numbers in case you don't have service for some reason. Also, be on the lookout for blue and yellow boxes labeled "CALL BOX" on the side of every freeway from which you can make calls. If you are ever lost or need help, ask people around you. San Diegans are known for their generosity and respect for others. They will do what they can to assist.

49. Shop To Your Heart's Content

There are tons of places to shop around the county. Westfield has numerous malls in the area, all of them fantastic with brand name stores and restaurants to enjoy. Malls to check out are North County Fair (newly renovated with a bowling alley), Fashion Valley (the high-end place to go), University Town Center (has an ice skating rink), Horton Plaza (in the middle of downtown), and Mission Valley. Other great places to shop are La Jolla Village (the Rodeo Drive of San Diego), Hillcrest (considered the LGBT community of San Diego which has some incredible, wonderful, unique, bizarre stores), Mira Mesa (huge shopping complexes), Seaport Village (a large variety of stores), and Coronado (Orange Ave. has a combination of high-end stores and souvenir shops).

50. Stop And Talk To People

San Diegans love meeting new people and interacting with others. The city is known for having very relaxed, welcoming people as its citizens. From riding the trolley, to walking the boardwalk, to ordering food, don't be surprised if people strike up a conversation with you with a smile on their face. If you have questions about the area, need any assistance, or simply want to meet new people and possibly make a friend, please take advantage of us friendly San Diegans. We love having visitors and want you to feel comfortable

> TOURIST

Please read other Greater than a Tourist Books.

Join the >Tourist Mailing List :
http://eepurl.com/cxspyf

Facebook:
https://www.facebook.com/GreaterThanATourist

Pinterest:
http://pinterest.com/GreaterThanATourist

Instagram:
http://Instagram.com/GreaterThanATourist

> TOURIST

Greater than a Tourist

Please leave your honest review of this book on Amazon and Goodreads. Thank you.

> TOURIST

Greater than a Tourist

You can find Greater Than a Tourist books on Amazon.

Tips

Discipline in the Music Classroom

Compiled by R. Louis Rossman

Published in partnership with
MENC: The National Association for Music Education
Frances S. Ponick, Executive Editor

Rowman & Littlefield Education
Lanham • New York • Toronto • Plymouth, UK

Published in partnership with
MENC: The National Association for Music Education

Published in the United States of America
by Rowman & Littlefield Education
A Division of Rowman & Littlefield Publishers, Inc.
A wholly owned subsidiary of The Rowman & Littlefield Publishing Group, Inc.
4501 Forbes Boulevard, Suite 200, Lanham, Maryland 20706
www.rowmaneducation.com

Estover Road
Plymouth PL6 7PY
United Kingdom

British Library Cataloguing in Publication Information Available

Library of Congress Cataloging-in-Publication Data

ISBN-13: 978-0-940796-60-7 (pbk. : alk. paper)
ISBN-10: 0-940796-60-0 (pbk. : alk. paper)

♾™ The paper used in this publication meets the minimum requirements of
American National Standard for Information Sciences—Permanence of
Paper for Printed Library Materials, ANSI/NISO Z39.48-1992.
Manufactured in the United States of America.

Foreword

MENC: The National Association for Music Education has created the TIPS series to provide music educators with a variety of ideas on a wide range of practical subjects. Each TIPS booklet is a compilation of methods, ideas, and suggestions that have been successful in the music classroom. MENC has designed this quick-reference series to be used as a starting point for creating and adapting projects for your particular situation.

TIPS: Discipline in the Music Classroom is designed for music teachers at all levels who would like some fresh ideas for maintaining discipline in the classroom or rehearsal room.

Table of Contents

Foreword i

Introduction 1

Classroom Control: Concepts and Components 3

The Teacher's Role 5

Planning and Management 9

    Using Resource Personnel 10

    Management Techniques for Performance Activities 11

    Management Techniques for Listening Activities 14

    Management Techniques for Creative Activities 15

Strategies 17

    Behavior Contracts 19

    Rules 22

An Environment for Learning...24

Acknowledgments...26

Introduction

Is the discipline in your classroom out of control? Gallup Poll respondents have consistently listed discipline as one of the highest ranking problems in schools. Teachers, administrators, school boards, and parents have been concerned with improving education for many years. One perennial topic is that of discipline. Even United States presidents have been asked to provide leadership in restoring authority in public schools: Former president Ronald Reagan cited the primary need to restore "good old-fashioned" discipline in the classroom. He also indicated that too many schools across the land do not give teachers the proper authority to even restore quiet in their classes.

When the authority of a teacher is undermined, newspaper headlines often appear that support a specific action taken by a teacher or by a student involved in a given incident. In either case, the implication that teachers and students have opposing interests is certain to cause turmoil both in the school and in the entire district.

Many educators have cited the demise in public school discipline during the past forty years as a primary factor in the decline in general literacy, social courtesy, and respect for public laws and integrity. They have further contended that firm discipline leads to sound habits for study and social interaction, which is important during students' formative years and during their individual social development. A lack of discipline, however, creates an undesirable attitude for study, social interaction, law and order, and achievement.

National groups, including the National Association of Secondary School Principals and the PTA, have issued agendas for improving schools, and stricter discipline continues to be one of the primary suggestions offered by these groups. Their findings indicate that extra time devoted to education should not consist of a higher concentration of similar programs, but that schools should offer alternative choices including extra work in the arts, foreign languages, or computer instruction. These groups also have stressed the importance of alternatives to homework and textbook assignments such as educational experiences in music rooms or laboratories.

Educational leaders, including superintendents, principals, and career counselors, have emphasized the parents' role as their children's first and most influential teachers. They have noted that many highly successful individuals do not claim extraordinary intelligence, but instead contend that accomplishment is often more dependent on hard work and self-discipline than on innate ability.[1]

Many students are discouraged by teachers, and discouraged children have difficulty learning. All too often, teachers point out what a student has done wrong rather than what he or she has done right. Mistakes are checked in red, but correct answers are unmarked. Students are usually evaluated by comparing their achievement with that of others rather than by judging their own achievements. Students should be permitted to make mistakes while they are learning: Mistakes are not failures; they are necessary steps in the process of true learning. It is important to use encouragement rather than praise; praise is a value judgment, based on competition, but encouragement is an approach that focuses regularly on effort. Finally, teachers may transmit encouragement to students by serving as appropriate role models, thereby encouraging self-discipline and preventing many discipline problems in the classroom.

* * *

1. William W. Wayson and Thomas J. Lasey, "Climates for Excellence: Schools That Foster Self-Discipline," *Phi Delta Kappan*, February 1984, 419–21.

Classroom Control:
Concepts and Components

Maintaining discipline in the classroom means maintaining order in the classroom, and order starts as a process in the teacher's mind. A teacher who has a well-ordered and disciplined mind will probably strive for a well-ordered and disciplined class.

Misbehavior is a symptom of other problems: Factors such as ambient temperature, late-arriving buses, and peer pressure need to be recognized. When correcting misbehavior, never associate punishment with schoolwork. Avoid physical force whenever possible; use alternative methods. (Your legal right to chastise rests with the common law of your local school district.) The discipline procedures of your classroom must be adjusted to individual differences among students.

* * *

Students want and have a right to active participation, as a class or through the class officers, in policy developments such as the formulation of class rules. Student misbehavior must not, however, jeopardize the learning environment of others through excessive talking or deliberate dropping of books and pencils.

* * *

Self-discipline by the students fosters a climate for excellence. Depersonalization, on the other hand, is the most frequent cause of disruptive behavior in schools. Discipline problems can be avoided by developing the kind of school pride that comes when staff members and students share common understandings and a sense that they are participating and producing. Problems can be avoided by developing the commitment and loyalty that undergird self-disciplined adherence to mutually accepted codes of conduct. Discipline problems are not avoided by manufacturing crises that promote punishment and often prejudice.

Symbols of identity and excellence need to be promoted to create a sense of belonging and responsibility among the students. Good school discipline is produced when the total school environment is created for this purpose, rather than when isolated practices are designed to deal specifically with discipline problems. Faculty and staff must emphasize

3

positive and preventive practices, focusing on causes rather than symptoms of unwanted behavior. We, as teachers, must further the development of good discipline by having faith in our own students and ourselves and by expending unusual amounts of energy to make this belief a reality. We should adopt the disciplinary practices that are necessary to meet our own needs and styles, but we must be sure to make our decisions for the benefit of the students.

* * *

We must consider other factors when attempting to foster good discipline in young students. Don Collins offered some suggestions about these factors.[2] He noted that a youngster who respects others respects himself or herself first. Student self-respect is not accomplished by being an overbearing, tyrannical, and unreasonable teacher: That approach often produces a submissive, polite, frightened, but deceitful child. It is better to have open rebellion on the surface than to force fear underground, storing up years of resentment and hatred that may erupt in young adulthood.

Students do not want a buddy; they want an adult who will act as a willing, honest, and successful guide no matter how much the students disagree with and "test" the guidance. The most successful teacher, therefore, is one who is patient, conscientious, and honest and who teaches with authority and kindness.

* * *

Remember that students are valuable individuals with a right to self-respect, pride, and dignity. They deserve to be treated with respect and politeness, and their personal integrity should not be questioned or attacked. Sarcasm and causing embarrassment are not appropriate and are often interpreted as ridicule by sensitive adolescents. To create a productive learning environment, you must establish the feeling that you and the students are working together in the learning process. Capitalize on the students' enthusiasm, conducting firm but fair rehearsals without using excessive strictness that results in an uncomfortable, less productive, and rigid classroom climate. You must be well prepared and enthused about teaching, possess the drive needed to lead and interact with the class effectively, and demonstrate a willingness to take the students' personal concerns into consideration. A confrontational attitude on your part is self-defeating.

* * *

2. Don Collins, "Singing Is the Gift. Discipline Is the Way. Making Music Is the Art," *The Actual Pitch* 3, no. 1, 1983, 6–7.

The Teacher's Role

You must be an effective communicator in the classroom. Many times discipline problems arise because a teacher has not been clear in conveying the message or has sent contradictory messages. Teachers need to coordinate their body language, speaking voice, eye contact, and wardrobe to create a convincing, but not confusing, impact on the learner.

* * *

Be assertive, but not hostile. Beginning with this attitude, you should cultivate enthusiasm and express it with your face, voice, and overall intensity. Vary the vocal inflection, dynamic level, and rate of speed at which you speak, but never talk too rapidly or move from one point to another too quickly, and never attempt to talk over noise. You can use a well-modulated voice to calm disruptive behavior, just as you can unknowingly spawn discipline problems with a high-pitched, strident voice. Try to increase the intensity of your speaking voice a little to give a greater sense of authority and command: Think in terms of speaking firmly to the student who is at the greatest distance from you. It is sometimes tempting to speak in a casual, conversational manner when it is more appropriate to speak authoritatively in an explanatory, inspirational, or questioning manner.

* * *

Learn to make maximum use of eye contact. If a student is beginning to lose attention, make more eye contact to ensure intensity and maintain this contact a little longer than usual. Also, remember that students enjoy having the teacher sit among them while another student goes to the front of the room and leads the class in a song, conducting experience, or exercise. Not only can your presence help establish in-tune singing in that section of the room, but it can avoid potential discipline problems.

* * *

When directing an ensemble, remember that directing is a language, and do not assume that students can understand this special language of signs—or that they are mind readers. Make certain that your directing techniques are adequate and consistent, especially in giving the exact point of attack for each specific note with the baton tip. Make a clear distinction between the "playing beats" and "nonplaying beats" of the baton, and keep all of your beats above and in front of the music rack so they are neither above nor below the players' line of vision. Your podium may be too high, or if you are tall, you may not need a podium. On the other hand, your music rack may be too low if it causes you to look down so that players cannot see your eyes (and you cannot use them to catch the attention of those who are being coached or cued). When it is necessary to stop a rehearsal for corrections, be specific about the section or individual that needs correcting, and give clear and definite directions about the point in the score at which the ensemble should resume playing.

* * *

Music teachers have all spent many years learning about the discipline of music. They have isolated themselves in practice rooms and have followed the leadership of conductors and professors. Now, in their own work, they must wield the baton as directors and provide (as teachers) the leadership necessary for their own students. This frequently means that teachers have to evaluate their leadership potential objectively and rise to the challenge, working hard at establishing musical as well as behavioral discipline.

In the early stages of our teaching careers, most of us emulate our directors or those teachers who taught us. When we try to control or motivate our students by using their techniques, we soon learn that we are walking down the primrose path. There is a very good reason for this: We do not have the same personalities as our teachers, nor do we relate to students in the same manner in which they did. We have our own personalities, and we relate to people in our own ways.

* * *

How do you motivate students? You look inside yourself and determine those characteristics in your personality that make you unique; then you develop, sharpen, mold, and hone those characteristics into the best possible combination. A dry wit, tremendous energy, a keen sense of humor, or maybe an effervescent personality are only a few of the valuable personality traits that you may identify, and you can use all of them

6

to motivate your students. Just remember that you are the only person in the world who is uniquely you, and capitalize on your strengths!

* * *

You must always treat your students consistently and considerately, giving clear lessons and assignments, establishing good classroom routines, and never playing favorites or gossiping with students. Don't fall into a pattern that includes unchanging methods, roll calls, or an emphasis on fact-oriented tests. In an ensemble, you as the director can avoid most of the discipline problems that might arise. Prepare for rehearsal by checking the score and parts for misprints or errors, learning the music beforehand, and developing a systematic plan. Then, start the rehearsal on time with an effective warm-up procedure. Always make sure that the players are ready before giving preparatory beats, and then give, in a consistent manner, two beats rather than one: This will ensure good rhythm on the attack.

In the event of mistakes in performance or in the score, encourage players to question passages that sound incorrect. Stop as infrequently as possible, and only stop for good reason. Then diagnose the problem quickly and accurately. Do not merely keep repeating the passage and hoping for a miracle. Avoid working too long on the problems of one section or of one player; if you do this, you will lose the interest and attention of the rest of the organization. Also, avoid working too long on a particular passage; if you do, you face a law of diminishing returns.

When restarting, make one decision about the point to begin. Avoid changing your mind and confusing the students with verbiage such as, "Let's start three measures before rehearsal letter M. . . no, let's make it seven measures before M. . . ." Before rehearsing, be sure that every measure is numbered on each player's part to avoid wasting time counting measures from rehearsal letters, because this practice makes it likely that players will not start at the correct place and causes confusion and irritation.

Avoid wasting time rehearsing complete passages when rehearsing "spots" would save time. Break down problems into their various factors, and drill each factor before putting them together for a good result.

Develop good testing procedures (especially visual testing) to spot those students who need help. Do not let players get set in bad habits and then shout at them, but be consistent and timely in correcting errors and faults. Use the chalkboard to clarify problems, and try to communicate fundamentals so that the students transfer the basic principles of musicianship from one work to another. This avoids wasting rehearsal time in learning each composition by rote. Teach the students to listen; they must be able to hear accurately and quickly. Finally, you must teach the students to be attentive to your direction and ensure that they can do so by checking the height and position of the students' music racks. If they are looking down or in the wrong direction, they cannot possibly respond to the indications that you give with the baton. Teach them to adjust the height and position of the music rack so that they can all see your eyes, facial expression, and motions, as well as the music. As soon as the students are watching you, it is your job to take advantage of their attention by communicating with them: "Get the music in your head, and keep your head out of the music."[3]

* * *

The following is a checklist for teacher self-assessment:

____ Organized	____ Has effective lessons
____ Establishes rules	____ Has sense of humor
____ Knows the students	____ Praises
____ Consistent	____ Predictable
____ Self-aware	____ Self-controlled
____ Self-assured	____ Knowledgeable
____ Sensitive	____ Sensible
____ Enthusiastic	____ Energetic
____ Sincere	____ Fair
____ Flexible	____ Friendly
____ Observant	____ Specific
____ Respects	____ Prevents

* * *

3. Adapted from "Ways in Which Discipline Problems Are Caused by the Director," *Kansas Music Review*, October–November 1969, 23.

9663 S

0005108**9663**

Inspected By: Angelica_Vazquez

Sell your books at sellbackyourBook.com!
Go to sellbackyourBook.com and get an instant price quote. We even pay the shipping - see what your old books are worth today!

Planning and Management

A creative and confident teacher with a well-planned lesson is a good deterrent to discipline problems in a music classroom. You must not equivocate regarding what is to be accomplished, the sequence of activities, and how to apply them. Plan both short- and long-range goals. (You may want to use visual outlines to increase the students' knowledge of your expectations.) You should establish realistic goals for each class session. Initially, provide broad suggestions and refine your goals during successive class sessions.

Activities should involve all segments of the class, even when they deal primarily with individuals. Your challenges should be achievable: Use methodologies that appeal to gifted and nongifted students. You must, however, be flexible enough to accommodate unexpected, legitimate changes in direction that a class might pursue because of classroom dynamics. You might, for example, design a lesson that compares the production of tone on reed instrument mouthpieces with that on brass instruments. If an attentive student asks about the mechanical aspects of changing pitch on brass instruments, you may want to alter your lesson plan to include a more comprehensive explanation of rotary and piston valves on brass instruments. An informed and knowledgeable teacher is capable of improvising properly in these situations and not allowing such tangents to undermine control of the class. When planning, therefore, you should always prepare activities that students will quickly grasp as well as activities that extend the lesson.

* * *

To maintain learning momentum, you must take care to organize and focus the class toward effective and positive discipline at the beginning, during, and at the close of the class. Anticipate students' arrival and greet them at the door with a smile and by name. Start promptly, but not early (or a prompt start for the next class may seem late). Be neat and organized—atmosphere and appearance set the stage. Be imaginative in your use of bulletin boards, lights, and physical setup, and monitor changes in the environment such as the ambient heat and the amount of activity outside your classroom windows. Do not allow any unrelated materials, such

9

as textbooks from other classes or notebooks, to distract the students in a music rehearsal. They should be shelved or stored before the rehearsal.

* * *

Ask yourself whether the classroom furniture and equipment is well ordered and whether the students are placed in seats that are beneficial to them. If needed, build a music cart so that you can have the equipment at hand when you need it. Both you and the students will respond to a productive environment in which the needs and functions of the class have been considered and in which an aura of purpose and order is apparent.

* * *

Minimize delays and disruptions (most telephone calls can be returned at another time), and keep the lesson moving. Maintain a sense of accountability; use a variety of questioning procedures and consistent evaluation. Monitor class attentiveness, and terminate lessons that seem too long. When planning your lessons, incorporate changes of mood by scheduling a change of pace every six to nine minutes.

* * *

Stress positive work rather than control. Plan lessons around your students' interests and aptitudes. Employ self-directed learning, in which the student takes the initiative and responsibility and the teacher provides activities and experiences that permit the student's achievement of personally set goals. When leading classroom discussions, avoid asking specific content questions early in the year; instead, focus on questions that involve thinking, feeling, and opinion.

* * *

Using Resource Personnel

When considering the use of resource personnel, you must first realize that you might be the only resource some students have to deal with problems in their lives, but do not hesitate to refer the students to professionals if necessary in individual instances. Talk to the principal about any serious problems, and make use of any special help available to you. The person you ask for advice will usually respect you for having the good judgment to ask, will be flattered by the implication that he or she is a wise person, and will develop a sense of contribution to your success. Try to develop a good relationship with a colleague with whom you can talk honestly about your fears, joys, and frustrations. Analyze the successful techniques of every teacher you know—both professors and colleagues—to broaden your perspective.

* * *

Management Techniques for Performance Activities

Choose your music carefully so that it is both interesting enough and easy enough for your students, and know the music well. It is best to memorize it so that you can maintain eye contact with students. If you play the accompaniments, be familiar enough with your part so that you can maintain frequent eye contact with the students. If your class is performing with a recording, know what is on the record: Know whether there is an introduction and how long it is, how many verses are recorded, and whether there are instrumental interludes between verses.

* * *

Announce, establish, and enforce efficient classroom routines that all ensemble members must follow. Plan procedures for distributing music books or song sheets. Make sure that you have enough parts so that no student is idle, and write the rehearsal order on the board so that students can organize materials when they arrive for class.

* * *

Use all instructional time for instruction and not for organizational activities. For example, set up chairs, stands, and equipment before the rehearsal period. Distribute and collect music before or after rehearsal time, not during the rehearsal. As much as possible, take care of non-instructional activities such as fundraising outside of the instructional time period. Establish and follow a regular procedure to indicate that the students' attention is required before beginning the rehearsal.

* * *

Plan procedures for assigning and distributing instruments, and determine what criteria you will use for choosing players. In elementary school groups, the class might be able to sing a familiar song while this is being done. If the students must move from one area of the classroom to another, determine whether it can be done in a musical context (such as moving one row of students for each phrase of music). Determine how the students will return to their seats. Establish a routine for what to do with instruments when they are not being played. "Mallets on the desk" or "place the instruments on the floor under your chair" are examples of routines that can be established.

11

Provide clear and concise directions. Establish a routine for starting a song, giving indications of pitch, tempo, and a starting point. When playing introductions, keep them short—one phrase. Students want to perform, not listen to you play. Musical (or movement) demonstrations are frequently more effective than verbal explanations.

* * *

You will encounter fewer discipline problems if you guide students to achieve independent performance goals. You must help students learn the music. Break down difficult sections into simple patterns, and plan a variety of ways to help students learn those patterns—through clapping, playing instruments, moving, or singing. Refer to notation whenever possible. Notation will help students become independent music learners, but they must be taught to read it. Return to a given musical selection on successive days. Perform with the students, but do not let them become dependent on your performance. Frequently stop singing or playing and listen to their performance. When using recordings, do not let the students become dependent on recordings for support. As students learn a song, decrease the volume of the record player. Remember that your goal is to help students become independent performers.

* * *

Use efficient methods: Any wasted time creates discipline problems. The time for working with individuals or sections must be kept very brief. If they need a lot of work, schedule a separate practice, but try to relate most of your instruction to the whole group. For example, if you are teaching a rhythmic pattern, teach it to everyone. Make the point that you want all the students to learn the whole composition—not just their own parts. Reinforce this point by asking the whole group a question or two about the sections that you work on individually. (How was this? What still needs to be done? How does this function in the composition? Can you hear this clearly when we all perform?)

When you must rehearse one section of the ensemble, try giving the other sections specific jobs. For example, you could say: "Sopranos, basses and tenors, I'll want to hear you read the rhythm in the tenor line on page 3, systems 1 and 2, on 'ta' and 'ti-ti' (or any rhythmic reading system) as soon as I finish with the altos." This not only keeps the nonsinging sections musically active; it continuously develops musicianship.

* * *

In a rehearsal, listen and analyze what is happening constantly so that when there is a pause, you can quickly direct the students' attention to a

12

particular problem. If you are slow to think and react, time is wasted and problems can arise.

* * *

Plan transitions from one activity to another. For example, highlight relationships between musical selections, or sequence activities so that the mood of the music can shape the overall mood of the class. A fast tempo song that includes physical movement may be a good way to create class unity after an exciting game at recess. Use a quiet song to get the class ready for a library activity.

Plan periods of rest within a period of strenuous activity. After working for ten minutes on a new song, sing a familiar song before moving to another new composition. After a period of working on a strenuous movement activity, have students sit on the floor and sing a quiet song before continuing the work with the movement.

Finally, plan an ending for the music lessons. Whenever possible, help students experience a feeling of accomplishment by combining a song with accompaniment or with movement. If musical satisfaction cannot be achieved through the particular music on which the class has been working, end the music lesson with the performance of a favorite song. Plan a "musical summary," using a phrase such as "Let's perform this song, noticing the stepwise melody, the triple meter, the ABA form, and the other learnings we discovered today."

* * *

Developing a strong leadership system within the music ensemble is an effective way to manage student behavior or misbehavior. With elected student officers, review ensemble policies and procedures. Even if the officers perceive the need for some slight change in a given policy, their acquiescence and participation signifies an acceptance by elected representatives of the policies and procedures governing behavior within the group. You may be able to carry this a step further by using the officers in an advisory capacity if a policy is broken.

Give leadership responsibility to as many students as practical. When individuals assume responsibility for some portion of the organization, they invest something of themselves in the outcome of that endeavor. Some potential leadership roles include squad leader (group of marching band members), part leader (in a chorus), section leader (such as second violin or third trumpet), stand leader (such as third stand of third clarinets), ensemble captain, sophomore class representative, band manager, or librarian. A leader must have something to lead, so be sure the leader is given specific areas of responsibility in the organization.

* * *

Maintaining order in the percussion section is a problem common to most instrumental ensembles. You can avoid some of these problems by assigning a principal player and an assistant principal player to each percussion part as needed. While the "principal" rehearses on the instrument, the assistant principal rehearses at his seat (or better yet, in a practice room). That way both will learn the part, and you have a backup player when someone is absent. Assign parts on each selection, and make an individual folder for each member of the section. Include a master sheet of all assignments in each folder.

Many beginning or intermediate instrumental compositions have no mallet parts. In these cases, assign percussionists to a mallet instrument and give them a copy of the oboe part to play. When you have too many percussionists for the parts required, select music for a percussion ensemble that requires the talents of the extra percussionists. With an appointed captain, they can go to a practice room to work on the ensemble while you rehearse the entire group. (This could also provide some music for the next Music Parents meeting!)

* * *

Management Techniques for Listening Activities

Know the music well, and be able to make one or two statements about each of the important musical aspects of the composition as well as about the composer, performer, or circumstances under which the music was written. Identify aspects of the music you want to convey to students, and know where to locate specific sections of the music on the record or tape.

Establish effective classroom routines. Plan procedures for grouping and seating students during listening. Plan procedures for passing out listening guides, call charts, and other materials, and then keep talking to a minimum; let the music do the communicating. Discussions should take place before and after the listening. There should be no talking while the record or tape is playing. Adjust the volume of the record or tape player to simulate a live performance. If the music is too soft, it will become background music; if it is too loud, listening will become uncomfortable. Turn the volume down when starting and stopping a record to avoid the "thud" or scratch of the needle being placed on the record.

* * *

Discipline problems can be avoided if you plan a way to introduce the music to the students by involving them as active listeners. Give, clearly and concisely, only the information that will help them meet the specific objectives of a particular lesson; then, in a few carefully worded statements, give students specific aspects for which they are to listen. Help students develop an adequate vocabulary for discussing music, but also make frequent use of traditional and graphic notation or physical movement; music is frequently difficult to describe with words. Question the students about the example, using both "open" and "closed" questions.

* * *

Model good listening behavior, showing the students that you approach listening as a pleasurable experience. Listen with the students, and avoid preparing materials for the next activity while the music is playing.

* * *

Management Techniques for Creative Activities

Predetermine which activities can be accomplished in large groups and which will require smaller groupings. Plan procedures for dividing the class into groups and for moving to group work areas. Identify a leader for each group. Avoid placement of two strong "leadership personalities" in the same group, and provide written instructions for group leaders when working in small groups.

* * *

Plan and define the parameters within which students are to work. Limit the sounds from which students will select their musical materials, restrict the aspects of sound (pitch, duration, timbre, or dynamics) that students are to explore, and establish realistic limitations on the length of the expected composition and the time to be spent on the activity. Provide opportunities for students to work on one composition over an extended period of time, such as fifteen minutes each day for a week, to make refinements in their compositions. You will need to use questioning techniques to help the students explore, invent, and organize sounds and to help them develop criteria and procedures for evaluating their own compositions.

* * *

Plan work methods for the students, including procedures for getting out and returning instruments and other materials and a hierarchy of activities (indicating what should be done first, second, third, and so on). Communicate all of your instructions and expectations clearly to students.

* * *

15

Establish a "frame of silence" around each composition by beginning and ending with at least five seconds of silence. Then, recognize the artistic qualities of the students' compositions. Reinforce the process rather than the product by giving verbal and nonverbal reinforcement to students who are efficiently working through the process of exploring, inventing, and organizing sound. Finally, you can provide a great deal of positive reinforcement by giving students opportunities to perform compositions in a concert-like atmosphere for other students and for adults.

* * *

Strategies

Affirmation is one of the most direct and effective disciplinary tools. Each student needs to know that he or she is accepted, even if, at times, his or her behavior is not. Parents and teachers can work together for the benefit of the student. If both agree on a plan to help a child alter behavior and work together in a team effort, much can be accomplished.

* * *

Consistency, routine, and organization will prevent or eliminate many discipline problems. Discipline is a positive matter and should be viewed as *motivation* rather than *controlled behavior*. Whenever, as a teacher, you decide you are going to "make your students behave," you may be on the road to failure. When you begin to look for ways to "turn the student on" to music, you probably are on the road to success.

* * *

Well-managed classrooms have few problems. The first step in managing your classroom is to learn the students' names thoroughly and quickly. To speed up the process, take pictures of each row, table, or section of students and make a seating chart to accompany the pictures (this works for all grade levels). With a Polaroid camera or the help of a quick-print developing company, you can develop the photographs and learn the students' names literally overnight. You can then post the pictures on the bulletin board as the focus of a display that will provide a source of interest and pride to the students.

* * *

Classroom discipline problems can be prevented by making sure that students see the value and importance of what they are learning. They should be actively involved in the learning process so that they are not diverted by extraneous incidents or undesirable personalities.

* * *

17

It takes a high energy level to motivate a group of students. Use short-term goals, set a pace that is as quick as appropriate for the students' level of maturity, and work with a sense of urgency. You must use class time efficiently and prepare lessons and materials carefully; however, you must allow for whatever lesson flexibility is warranted by a given situation. Prepare lesson plans that are interesting for yourself as well as for the students. This will help motivate you and give you the incentive to work through the plan with the students. If students are frustrated, embarrassed, bored, or defeated—to name just a few problems—they will mirror their attitudes in the classroom. Anticipate and adjust any behavior that promotes those negative emotions.

* * *

Maintain consistent and high-level expectations for student behavior. Create a sense of individual responsibility and accountability: Give students written tests about the music they are rehearsing, and use audio-cassettes to create a permanent record of accomplishment for each individual. Students often interpret "drill" as a negative word: Use words such as "game" or "challenge," and create multiple ways of practicing a concept to avoid its repetition in the same way dozens of times.

* * *

In elementary choral classes, reinforce good performances with a variety of verbal and nonverbal reinforcement for both individual and group performances. Provide opportunities for the class to "show off" their performing skills by performing for another class or for a parents' group. Tape-record students' performances on a good-quality recorder so they can hear themselves. Exchange tapes of favorite songs with a class in another school.

* * *

When a K–1 child "tests" your disciplinary measures, take the student aside the first two or three times disruptive behavior occurs and whisper the correction and consequences to the child. If corrections are consistently made audibly, a young child may capitalize on them as attention getters. Whispering to a child may forestall the repetition of overt misbehavior.

When you are tempted to completely "blow your top," count to ten, and try to act as unemotionally and objectively as possible. Teachers must never lose their tempers. They may sometimes seem to become angry, but they must *never* actually lose control of their emotions. Students sometimes intentionally push teachers to lose their tempers just to create excitement in the class.

* * *

One way to handle discipline for young children is to make use of a "stop and go" sign. Instead of raising your voice, try holding up the "stop" side of the sign when the volume of noise or disruptive behavior takes place. If one student needs to be disciplined, walk down the aisle and hold the sign directly in front of him or her. This can be a good alternative to an audible reprimand.

When young children are moving into formation for a singing game or dance, precede the action with the word "freeze." Then whisper "tiptoe to the dancing circle" to reduce running and shoving. Minimize talking and disruptive behavior as students enter the music classroom by pinning strips of paper on the bulletin board nearest the door and having each child pull a slip as he or she enters the room. Write a notated melodic, rhythmic, or other musical problem on each slip along with a number, and sometime during the class (perhaps when least expected) use the number to call on someone to solve the musical problem. Assign points for each correct answer, and let those points accrue to a total for that row or side of the room.

* * *

Behavior Contracts

Behavior contracts are tools that can aid teachers in classroom management. Contracts are an integral part of several discipline strategies used in today's schools, including social discipline, behavior modification, and assertive discipline. The contract serves as a signed agreement between the teacher and the student for students and, in certain situations, for the parents. It includes the specific reinforcement or punishment that will result from successful performance or failure to meet the stipulations of the contract. Contracts provide the students with the structure that will encourage them to behave in an acceptable and appropriate manner.

When establishing a contract with a student or a group, use the following steps:

1. Determine or select the behavior that must be changed.
2. Specify clearly what the desired behavior should be.
3. Negotiate with the student the rewards or consequences to be established.
4. Specify how you will monitor and evaluate the behavior.
5. Set a time for the length of the contract. (You and the student may

wish to set a date before the completion of the contract on which you can evaluate the student's progress and, if appropriate, rewrite the contract.)

6. Put the contract in writing.

7. Have all concerned parties sign.

Contracts can be used to improve behavior problems with individuals or groups or as a means of setting performance goals for both individuals and groups. Individual contracts are used to help students with problems that are more serious than the "normal" range of troublesome classroom behavior. They can be presented in a variety of formats (see the suggested form on page 21). With the elementary school child, the steps and format can be simplified; with older students, the details should be very clearly defined and stated. Do not arbitrarily impose a contract on a student, but negotiate and give the student an opportunity to reflect on his or her behavior and the means by which it can be improved.

You must select reinforcement and punishment techniques that are not only obtainable, but are a normal part of the school program. These techniques should reflect school system procedures and state law. You might reward students for success with a contract by selecting a study topic that is of great personal interest to the students, verbally commending their accomplishment, and providing a written record of their attainment. The written record can be sent to all appropriate persons, such as the students, parents, and the school principal. When setting up and carrying out a contract, you must focus on positive, correct behavior as much as possible. If you believe that the student's parents should be aware of the problem and can be of assistance, invite them to be part of the final agreement.

Group contracts may be needed to correct a problem that exists throughout a class, such as getting to class or rehearsal late, excessive talking, playing of instruments at inappropriate times during class, and other off-task behaviors. The teacher and class usually develop the contract during a class meeting; the teacher approaches the situation by stating, "Okay, we have a problem. What can we do to correct it?" Again, as in the individual contract, the teacher should not impose the contract on the students but should direct the group so that the students perceive the problem and determine a method for improvement. The value of social or peer pressure in this group approach to contracting is a strength of the technique. There are, however, some dangers inherent in this type of contract: Some students may intentionally break the contract, those who are behaving may be resentful of the contract, and it may be difficult to find a reward that is attainable and that will be effective for all.

Goal setting is a helpful technique for individuals or classes that lack direction or behavioral consistency. There is no real punishment used, but reinforcement results if the specified goals are met. Again, students' input is important. They should brainstorm possible goals for a week, a month, or longer. One teacher used this method to improve sight-reading skills in band. The students identified the long-range goals and several short-term goals, and cooperatively they planned with the teacher the techniques to be used to improve their skills. The payoff could then be a free day or an extracurricular activity. If you give this kind of direction and focus to study, you may forestall many behavior problems.

If you have not tried contracts in your management strategies, do so. They provide a very clear, definite structure, one that encourages students to assume their share of responsibility in improving the classroom environment.

Sample Behavior Contract

Contract between _____ and _____ Date _____
                        (student)   (teacher)

Description of behavior problem:

Description of desired behavior:

Plan for behavior change:

Rewards or consequences of contract:

Monitoring and evaluation of contract:

Comments:

Signed _____ Date _____
                        (student)

Signed _____ Date _____
                        (teacher)

Copies to: _____

            _____

Rules

The combination of techniques that you use to maintain control in the classroom is a personal matter, and it will depend on your own strengths and weaknesses and the specific situation. The best methodologies emphasize the most unobtrusive techniques so that good control becomes an effortless result of your teaching style. Your effectiveness as a teacher and the level of satisfaction you achieve will depend largely on your skill in adapting relevant rules to each new situation.

* * *

Establish the rules by explaining the reasons for their implementation: the practical reasons and the benefits in terms of accomplishment for the group and the individual. Indicate problems in a tangible way: They should have an effect on grades or result in notes or calls to parents. Involve students in formulating clear rules, formal and informal. Phrase these few but firm rules in positive ways, enforce them fairly and consistently, and use visual and oral reminders as reinforcement throughout the year. When making corrections, be specific and explain how to improve behavior, leaving the students' egos intact. It is your purpose to help the students alter their behavior, not to belittle them.

* * *

If you are a less experienced teacher, consider the similarities and differences between natural energy and disruptive behavior. The comparison will help you develop a better sense of what to ignore and what to address. Examining the alternatives often leads to the realization that doing less is sometimes far better than doing more.

* * *

Teachers who have an established sequence for maintaining discipline generally accomplish their lesson objectives. One such sequence for dealing with a misbehaving student might be:

1. While keeping the class activity moving, make direct eye contact with the student.
2. If misbehavior continues, keep the class activities moving while standing behind the student. Your physical proximity can be a powerful deterrent to a student with mischief in mind. Often walking slowly to stand a moment or two by a chair or desk is all that is necessary to correct a problem. Remember, however, that a larger, more intimidating physical presence does not automatically create good

discipline. It is rather the size of the mental strength and determination of the teacher: Mental toughness is a marvelous attribute.

3. If the message doesn't get through, keep the class activities moving while switching the student with another, telling the problem student that he or she sings or works better in the new position.

4. If correction is still needed, give a short admonition, making your words quick, quiet, and (depending on the problem) potent. Avoid repeated reprimands: Tell the student that he or she has forced the teacher to speak and to see the teacher after class.

5. As a last resort, move the student outside the "circle of learning." The after-class conference should allow the student to explain to the teacher why such a meeting was necessary. Having the student write and sign a statement about why he or she was singled out often helps children in the upper grades.

* * *

Don't make threats that you will not or should not carry out. Penalties should be addressed in the context of the formulation of rules, before the need arises. When inappropriate behavior occurs, identify and challenge it specifically, but build self-respect, group pride, and confidence with positive reinforcement when it is genuinely deserved.

* * *

Students need to learn about proper behavior in a musical setting as well as about music itself. Teach them how musicians treat one another personally, approach one another's music, rehearse, and behave at concerts. Music teachers share with other faculty members and parents the responsibility to teach general social behaviors to their students, who are citizens of the school, the community, and the world.

* * *

An Environment for Learning

The primary goal of a teacher is to manage the classroom so that an environment for learning is maintained. The appropriate environment for learning music may be somewhat different from the environment for learning other subjects. Being knowledgeable about the art and science of music itself makes one secure and eager to teach it to one's students. Students unfailingly sense this strength and respond to it.

The best discipline device is to be well prepared for every rehearsal and class presentation. A teacher who is confident, enthusiastic, and excited about the subject matter and who has a plan for sharing a love for music will have many fewer problems than one who is hesitant, lethargic, and "just doing a job." Keeping the rehearsal or lesson moving ahead without noticeable gaps and pauses, during which the minds of the students can wander off to other things, can prevent many discipline problems. Try to remember these aphorisms:

- Good pacing produces progress and prevents problems.
- Keep the score in your head and your head out of the score.
- An ounce of prevention is worth a pound of cure.
- Most people don't plan to fail, they just fail to plan.
- Plan your work, then work your plan, and you will have fewer discipline problems.

It is much wiser to use one's time in preparation than to spend it dealing with students who misbehave because of boredom or lack of focus on the subject. When a problem does arise, act in a manner that is fair, consistent, direct, and immediate. Excessive harshness will have an eventual backlash effect on the teacher. Playing favorites is always a mistake. Make direct eye contact with the student or students concerned with a look that says, "I am in charge and I expect your cooperation and respect," and you'll usually get it. If at all possible, deal with the problem when it occurs; problems have a way of worsening when left to fester. When you develop a reputation for fairness, consistency, directness, and immediacy, the students will be unlikely to create problems in your rehearsals or in your classroom. Then you will be free to concentrate on the important aspect of your job: sharing beauty through significant music.

Worthwhile and significant music will also result in fewer discipline problems. The use of music that is ephemeral in nature elicits a corresponding response—a response of only passing interest. Bach, Beethoven, Brahms, and Bernstein, for example, require concentration and constant effort, which is paid back in an aesthetic response. Cheap and tawdry music that has no deep and soul-fulfilling qualities will not hold the attention of young people for long. You are not an entertainer, but an educator. Remember and take pride in that title: The music teachers that are most effective in maintaining discipline in the classroom or rehearsal room are those who are most effective in educating our youth in the rigors and delights of music.

* * *

Acknowledgments

Koste Belcheff, director
School of Music
Ohio University, Oxford

Don L. Collins, founder and director
The Cambiata Vocal Music
Institute of America
Conway, Arkansas

Keith Dearborn
Associate professor of music
Bowling Green State University
Bowling Green, Ohio

Carole Delany, professor of music
California State University, Sacramento

Robert L. Erbes, area chair
Music Education
Michigan State University
East Lansing

Roy E. Ernst
Chair and professor of music education
Eastman School of Music
Rochester, New York

Max Ervin, MENC life member
Tuscon, Arizona

Kathleen Gjerdingen
Assistant professor of music
California State University, Fullerton

Robert H. Klotman
Professor emeritus of music
Indiana University, Bloomington

Sally Monsour
Professor of music education
Georgia State University, Atlanta

Arnold Penland, Jr.
Professor of music and associate dean
University of Florida, Gainesville

Carroll Rinehart
Visiting professor (retired)
Univeristy of Arizona, Tuscon

R. Louis Rossman
Chair and professor of music education
Morningside College, Sioux City, Iowa

James Saker
Director of university bands
University of Nebraska at Omaha

Keith Thompson
Professor of music
Valdosta State College
Valdosta, Georgia

Leonard Van Camp
Director of choral activities
Southern Illinois University
Edwardsville

William Wayson
Professor of education
Ohio State University, Columbus

Sister Lorna Zemke
Chair and professor of music
Silver Lake College
Manitowoc, Wisconsin

26

1095-3M-10/98